Cricut Mini:

Guide for beginners, Design Space,Cricut Air 2,Accessories and Materials.A Complete Technical Guide to Mastering with your Machine.

Technical Examples.

Table of Contents

Introduction

elcome to the last Cricut master guide. This guide will explain to you everything that needs to be known in order to start creating your best cut-up work. From the choice of the machine to the choice of materials; from the blade to the choice of the mats. The first part of this guide will cover the basics for Cricut design.

How to use Cricut's official software to create perfect presents for your friends or family, create arms, earrings, necklace and decorations at home. In addition, you can create personalized T-shirts, personalized cups and even dog tags

The first thing is: what is a Cricut machine? A Cricut is a cutting machine that can cut several different materials for your craft projects like paper, vinyl, and cardstock. Some Cricut machines can even cut thin wood, leather, fabric and more.

How that work? You can connect a Cricut to your computer wirelessly, create or download designs onto your computer, and then send them to your Cricut for cutting. Cricut has software called Design Space (available for Windows, mac & smart phone) that allows you to create and import designs to cut with your machine. The Cricut houses a tiny blade (or rotary cutter, or pen, or scoring tool) inside. Once you have a design ready to cut in Design Space, you can fasten your desired material onto a 12-inch-wide cutting mat, send your design from your computer to your Cricut wirelessly, and then load your material into your machine. With the press of a button, your project will begin cutting.

MACHINE

Cricut Joy

Just like full-size Cricut machines, Cricut Joy cuts and writes for you. It can cut 50+ materials, including materials you probably already have at home (copy paper, construction paper, etc.), popular crafting materials (iron-on, vinyl, Infusible Ink, etc.), and new Smart Materials, for super-easy, super-long cuts without a cutting mat. It's the perfect companion to any Cricut machine and a great way to dip your toe into DIY.

For space savers and people on the move

If you live in an apartment, a tiny house, or just love the simplicity of small, Cricut Joy will fit right in. Literally. It fits in a cubby, looks great on a counter, packs away easily, and sets up instantly.

For extra-long project people

Cricut Joy may be small enough to hold in the palm of one hand, but with Smart Materials, it can cut continuous shapes up to 4 inches wide and 4 feet long or make repeated cuts up to 20 ft long.

For last minute maker

We mentioned that Cricut Joy sets up instantly, which is particularly helpful when you're busy. It also works with new pre-scored Insert Cards, so you can bust out a custom card right before an event, a birthday bash, or a baby shower without breaking a sweat.

You'll also find lots of new projects in Design Space made specifically for Cricut Joy that take just about 15 minutes. If you're tight on time, this little beauties for you.

For avoid and not-so-avoid organizers

Some of our favourite Smart Materials for Cricut Joy are Smart Label™ Paper and Smart Label Vinyl. They make organizing quick, easy, and fun. Cricut Joy writes directly on Smart Label in any font, cuts it into any shape you say, and all that's left to do is for you to peel and stick.

Cricut Explorer Air 2

With the flexibility to cut a wide range of craft materials and the precision to deliver exactly what you need, the best-selling Cricut Explore Air 2 cutting machines make DIY easy, fun, and – dare we say – amazing.

For popular materials lover

Cricut Explore Air 2 is our best-selling machine for a reason! It cuts 100+ materials, including vinyl, iron-on, cardstock, and backed fabric.

For full-width project

The "biggest" difference between Cricut Joy and full-size machines is … size. Reach for Cricut Explore Air 2 or Cricut Maker when you need to cut anything wider than 4.25 inches, up to 12 inches.

For speedy makers

If you're in a hurry or just like to make the most of your time, you'll love Fast Mode, for up to 2X faster cutting and writing. It doubles your speed when working with popular materials like vinyl, iron-on, and cardstock. Both Cricut Maker and Cricut Explore Air 2 have Fast Mode.

For colour-obsessed crafters

One of our favourite things about Cricut Explore Air 2 is the wide variety of hues it comes in, from Flamingo Pearl and Wild Rose to Emerald, Peacock, Peach Kiss, and Cherry Blossom.

If you like to express your creativity by color-coordinating your craft room, Cricut Explore Air 2 just may be the machine for you.

Cricut Maker

Cricut Maker as all of the same amazing features as Cricut Explore Air 2, plus 10X the cutting power, making it our most versatile smart cutting machine.

For next level makers

Cricut Maker offers more tools, more materials, and more possibilities. It cuts 300+ materials (more than any other Cricut machine), from the most delicate paper to the tough stuff like leather and basswood.

For creative crafters who crave more

With its expandable suite of tools, including Knife Blade (for thicker, denser materials), Rotary Blade (for backed AND unbacked fabric), and the QuickSwap family of tools (for scoring, engraving, debossing, and adding decorative effects), Cricut Maker lets you take on practically any project.

For dimensional DIYers

Because it can cut thicker, denser materials, Cricut Maker is perfect for creating structural elements for 3D projects, including models, decor, and more.

For sewing enthusiast

If you sew or think you might ever want to learn, Cricut Maker can help with one of the most difficult and tedious parts, marking and cutting pattern pieces. You can even upload your own sewing patterns.

For savvy quilters

Quilters love Cricut Maker for cutting out appliqué and quilt pieces with precision so they can focus on the fun stuff.

For the sleek & stylish

Cricut Maker has a streamlined look that comes in 5 sophisticated hues (Champagne, Blue, Rose, Mint, and Lilac) with a shimmery metallic finish.

Blades

lades allow your Cricut machine to cut all of your projects. However, and depending on the types of materials you want to work with, you'll need a different kind of blade.

Each one of the blades has different superpowers and can cut different materials. Failing to use the right blade can damage your materials, or even the blade itself.

You don't NEED to worry about this though, because before you are going to cut a specific project, the Cricut Design Space software will tell you WHAT blade you need with any material.

Type of blades:

- Fine **Point blade** – Gold/Silver
- Deep **Point blade** – Black
- Bonded **Fabric blade** – Pink
- Foil **Transfer Kit** – Blue
- Rotary **blade** – only works with the Cricut Maker – Silver
- Knife **blade** – only works with the Cricut Maker – Silver
- Quick **Swap Perforation blade** – only works with the Cricut Maker – Silver

- Quick **Swap Wavy blade** – only works with the Cricut Maker – Silver

- Quick **Swap Debossing tip** – only works with the Cricut Maker – Silver

- Quick **Swap Engraving tip** – only works with the Cricut Maker – Silver

- Quick **Swap Scoring Wheel tips** – only works with the Cricut Maker – Silver

- Cricut **Joy Fine Point Blade** – Silver with a white top – Cricut Joy Only

Cricut blade anatomy

Cricut blades are exceptionally well designed and you can feel the quality of the materials once you are holding them in your hands. They are beautiful and do their job to perfection!

Besides, colours and functionality when you see a picture of one particular blade what you are seeing is not just the blade itself, but also the housing.

- **Housing:** is what holds the blade in place. When your blade is due for a change, you don't need to change the housing.

- **Drive Housing:** This type of housing is specifically designed for the Cricut Maker only, and they differ from standard housing blades because they have a golden top gear. The Cricut Adaptive Tool System drives these gears. Drive

Housing blades come with a plastic cover that should be left at all times to keep the gears clean.

- **Blade:** blades look somewhat similar to a small nail, and are inserted inside the housings. Blades can be replaced when cuts are not as sharp as they used to be. **Note:** blades for drive housing look all different.

What are the different types of Cricut Blades and What can they cut?

Right now, there are seven different blades and three different tips available. All nine tools can be used with the Cricut Maker, but only three of them can be used with the Cricut Explore Family Machine.

Fine Point Blade

The Fine Point blade is the most common, and it comes with all of the Cricut Machines. It's made out of German Carbide, which an extremely durable and high-quality material most commonly used for cutting tools materials.

This blade is perfect for making intricate cuts, and it's designed to cut medium-weight materials. It used to be silver, but it now comes in a beautiful golden color.

It works with any of the Cricut Explore Family machines and the Cricut Maker.

Note: Besides color (from silver to gold) there's no difference between the housings silver and gold housings, including the blade there's inside it when you initially purchase your machine.

However, when you purchase a replacement blade for the Cricut Maker/Explore ALWAYS MAKE SURE that you purchase the blade with the white cap. The grey cap it's for older Cricut machine models.

What Materials can I cut with the Fine Point blade?

- Printer Paper
- Vinyl: Glitter vinyl, printable, outdoor, holographic
- Iron-on or also HTV (Heat transfer vinyl)
- Cardstock
- Washi Tape
- Parchment Paper
- Vellum
- Canvas
- Light Chipboard
- Faux Leather (Paper Thin)

Deep Point Blade

If you need to cut thicker materials, the Deep Point blade will be your best friend. You can use it with any of the Cricut Explore Family machines or Cricut Maker!

The angle of this blade is so much steeper – 60 degrees compared to 45 degrees for the fine point blade – This allows the blade to penetrate and cut intricate cuts in thick materials.

The color of this blade is black and must be used with its respective housing. And by that, I meant that you can't interchange other blades like Fine Point and Bonded Fabric.

What Materials can I cut with the Deep Point blade?

- Craft Foam
- Aluminum Foil
- Genuine Leather
- Metallic Leather
- Magnetic Sheet – 0.6mm
- Corrugated Paper

Bonded Fabric Blade

The Bonded Fabric blade is like the Fine Point Blade, but it's color-coded so you only use it with fabric. To have a better experience when cutting fabric, don't use this blade paper, or vinyl.

There's a big caveat with this blade though. The fabric you are going to cut needs to be bonded to a backing material.

"Backing" is a type of material – like heat & bond – that you need to adhere – bond – to your fabrics so you can cut with this blade; hence the name Bonded Fabric blade.

If you don't bond your fabrics properly, you risk tearing apart and stretching out your materials, and you might also damage your mat.

Not fun, right?

This blade is compatible with the Explore Family Machines and Cricut Maker, the color is pink and can be used with the Fine Point blade Housing and with the Pink Fabric Mat.

What Materials can I cut with the Bonded Fabric blade?

ALL of these materials need to be bonded.

- Oil Cloth
- Silk
- Polyester
- Denim
- Felt
- Burlap
- Cotton

Foil Transfer Kit (New)

The "Foil Transfer Kit" allows you to create beautiful and crisp foil effects on your projects.

It's compatible with the Cricut Maker and any of the Explore family machines.

with iron-on you don't have the intricacy that the "Foil Transfer Kit" has.

This kit is 3 tools in 1; to best suit your project, Cricut has a fine, medium, and bold tips.

Here are some of the materials you can use when working with the "Foil transfer kit."

- Cardstock
- Deluxe Paper
- Pearl Paper
- Vellum
- Printable Vinyl
- Printable Sticker Paper
- Matboard
- Poster Board
- Copy Paper
- Photo Paper
- Faux Leather

Rotary Blade (Only Cricut Maker)

The Rotary blade is fantastic and it's driven by the Adaptive Tool System, that's why it's only compatible with the Cricut Maker Machine.

The drive housing for this blade isn't interchangeable with other blades. For you to change the blade itself, you need a particular kit.

The Rotary blade cuts through, pretty much, any fabric. And the best of all, you don't need any backing material to stabilize the fabric on the mat. That alone should get you super happy!

This blade also comes with the Cricut Maker (this is a big deal because you usually have to buy these sorts of tools separately or in a bundle) and can only be used with the Fabric Grip Mat.

Although this blade is very cool and potent, it does have a small restriction. The image or project size you are trying to cut should be at least 3/4 of an inch (19 mm). Cutting smaller projects will result in shortening the blade's life.

What Materials can I cut with the Rotary Fabric blade?

- Bamboo Fabric
- Bengaline
- Canvas
- Cashmere
- Chiffon
- Corduroy
- Cotton
- Denim
- Felt
- Fleece
- Gauze
- Silk
- Lycra
- Microfiber
- Nylon

Knife blade (Only Cricut Maker)

This knife blade is one of a kind, and it's only compatible with the Maker Machine.

The projects you can cut with this baby are just amazing. You can create wood signs for your home, boxes, extremely sturdy cake toppers and more.

The Purple or StrongGrip Mat is the mat you should be using with this blade. Sometimes that mat it's not even enough for you to keep the materials in place, especially if you are cutting wood.

If you need to add extra grip because of the material you are using, use painter's tape on the edges of it to secure it to the mat.

The drive housing for this blade isn't interchangeable with other blades.

What Materials can I cut with the Knife blade?

- Tooling Leather
- Balsa – 1/16 in & 3/32 in
- Basswood – 1/16 in & Basswood – 1/32 in
- Heavy Chipboard – 2.0mm
- Matboard 4 Ply

Quick Swap Tips and Blades (Only Cricut Maker)

Unlike the rest of the blades that have a different housing, The Quick Swap system allows you to use five different tools (2 blades, and 3 tips)

- Scoring Tip
- Engraving Tip
- Debossing Tip
- Wavy Blade

- Perforation Blade

Let's see a little bit more about all of these tools:

Perforation Blade

This particular blade will allow you to create projects with a tear finish. With this tool, a new world of possibilities has open. You can create coupons, raffle tickets, etc.!

Some of the materials you'll be able to use with this blade are:

- Corrugated Cardboard
- Metallic Poster Board
- Cardstock Glitter
- Cardstock Heavy Cardstock
- Felt
- Craft Foam
- Glitter Craft Foam
- Iron-On
- Faux Leather (Paper Thin)
- Tooling Leather – 2-3 oz. (0.8 mm)
- Vellum
- Plastic
- Acetate
- Foil Acetate

Wavy Blade

Instead of cutting on straight lines like the rotary or fine point blade, this tool will create wavy effects on your final cuts.

Getting curved lines in Design Space is quite complicated, so this tool will come in handy if you like these sorts of effects.

Gift Tags, banners, cards, envelopes, and unique vinyl decals are some of the projects that will benefit from this tool.

Some of the materials you can cut with this blade:

- Heavy Cardstock
- Corrugated Cardboard
- Foil Poster Board
- Kraft Board
- Metallic Poster Board
- Poster Board
- Glitter Cardstock
- Cotton Denim
- Flannel
- Fleece Fusible Fleece

Engraving Tip

The Engraving Tip is something that many crafters have been waiting for! With this tool, you'll be able to engrave a wide variety of materials.

Do you have a dog? What about making a dog tag! You can create monograms on aluminium sheets or anodized aluminium to reveal the silver beneath.

Here are some of the materials you'll be able to use with this blade:

- Anodized Aluminium
- Brass
- Bronze
- Stainless Steel
- Faux Leather (Paper Thin)
- Garment Leather – 2-3 oz. (0.8 mm)
- Genuine Leather
- Tooling Leather
- Vellum
- Acetate Foil
- Acetate

Debossing Tip

This tip will push the material in, and it will create beautiful and detailed designs. The debossing will bring your projects to a whole new level because of the detail you can now add to your designs.

Just imagine debossing a beautiful gift box with flowers, hearts, stars, etc.! You can also make 3D Cards and monograms!

Here's a list of some of the materials you'll be able to use with this tool:

- Foil Poster Board
- Heavy Chipboard – 2.0 mm
- Kraft Board
- Light Chipboard – 0.37 mm
- Matboard 4 Ply

- Metallic Poster Board
- Poster Board
- Foil Acetate
- Vellum
- Faux Leather (Paper Thin)
- Genuine Leather
- Tooling Leather
- Craft Foam Glitter Cardstock
- Heavy Cardstock
- Balsa – 1/16" (1.6 mm)
- Balsa – 3/32" (2.4 mm)

Scoring Wheel (Tip 01 and 02)

The Scoring Wheel is a tool that allows you to create beautiful, edgy, and crispy folds on your materials.

To give you the best results, Cricut has designed The Scoring Wheel with two different Tips, 01 and 02. Depending on the material you select, Design Space will suggest you the tip you need.

Tip 01: It is ideal for light materials such as print paper, regular cardstock, etc.

Tip 02: It is ideal for heavy and coated materials such as chipboard, glitter cardstock, metallic poster-board, etc.

Here are some of the materials you can use with this tool:

- Corrugated Cardboard
- Damask Chipboard
- Flat Cardboard

- Foil Kraft Board

- Heavy Chipboard – 2.0 mm

- Kraft Board

- Cardstock

- Foil Acetate

- Plastic Packaging

- Copy Paper

- Corrugated Paper

Cricut Joy Blades

The Cricut Joy only has a "Fine Point Blade." The blade housing has a white cap, and the blade itself it's quite different from any other blades.

The Cricut Joy Blade is not interchangeable; therefore, you need to use its respective housing.

Here are some of the materials you can cut with this blade:

- Smart Iron-On and Vinyl (Without a Cricut Mat)

- Copy Paper

- Cardstock

- Insert Cards with a Card Mat.

- Writable Vinyl

- Corrugated Cardboard

- Glitter Cardstock

- Foil Poster Board

Swapping housings

The Fine Point blade and the Bonded Fabric blade can use the same housing. Also, the **QuickSwap** tools can use the same housing, so if you already own one, from now on, you only need to get the tip or blade.

The other three remaining blades (Deep Point, Rotary, Knife) can only be used with their respective housing.

Buying blades

You can buy the blades from craft store, Walmart and the official cricut website

How long does the Cricut Blade Last?

Although Cricut blades are made to last for a reasonable amount of time, there comes a time where replacing the blade is necessary.

The blade's life depends on the kind of materials you are working with, how often you use them, and of course how you care for them.

For instance, paper and cardstock are harder on the blades than a much smoother material like vinyl is. So, if paper is your jam, then you'll go through blades more often.

Blades that cut through really thick materials like the Deep Point blade and, especially, the Knife blade need to be replaced more often because of the pressure that the blade needs to execute to get smooth and clean cuts.

You'll know you have to replace the blades when your cuts are dull and not as sharp as they used to be.

How to replace Cricut Blades?

The Fine Point, Deep Point, and Bonded Fabric are very easy to change. Just press the top of the blade, remove it with your hands and insert the new blade with the housing upside down.

The other blades – Rotary and Knife, are a little bit trickier.

How to Care for your Cricut Blades

Caring for your Cricut blades will increase their life. Blades and housings are quite the investment, so make sure you are doing your best to care for them at all times.

Here are a couple of tips for you to take care of your precious blades.

The best way to care for your blades is by using them with the right materials. It can be tempting to try to cut something thicker with the fine point blade if you don't have the Deep Point one.

However, not only your project won't be appropriately cut, but you will also add extra wear and tear to the blade.

Make sure to keep the plastic cover for blades – and also scoring wheel – that has a drive housing. This cover protects the gears of the housing. When you remove the cover, you are exposing the blade & housing to small particles like hair and dust.

Put them away when they are not in use.

How to Store your Cricut Blades

The Compartments inside the Cricut Machines are specifically designed to hold your blades – They thought of everything – For the replacement blades there's a metallic magnet that will keep them in place at all times.

The Cricut Maker has even more storage for you to keep the blades in place!

However, you decide to store them, make sure to put them way far away from your children's – or anyone else that doesn't know that's a blade – reach.

Frequent Cricut Blades Problems

There might be a point where you'll feel frustrated about your blades.

Maybe your blades are not cutting well, dragging the materials, cutting too deep, or simply not cutting at all!

Most of these problems can be solved by checking out your settings, especially if you modified them in the past to cut a custom material.

Maybe your mats are not stabilizing the material correctly, and you need to change them, or perhaps it's time for you to replace the blade.

Mats

"Cricut Mat" is the surface where you cut all of your projects. Right now, there are four different types of mats, Light Grip (blue), Standard Grip (green), Strong Grip (purple), and Fabric (pink).

Depending on the materials that you are working with, you will need a different mat.

If you don't use the correct mat for your project, you risk running your materials and then have a tough time removing them from the mat.

Cricut mats are sticky, and the level of stickiness dictates how secure the grip is. The stronger the grip, the heavier the material (like chipboard or thick card stock) you can cut, and the lighter the grip the thin or lightweight materials (like regular paper and vinyl), you can cut.

Mats are flexible, and this very useful because you can bend it to get out projects that are hard to remove otherwise.

Protective cover

A new Cricut mat will always have a transparent cover that protects the surface of the mat.

Outer Mat

This part of the mat doesn't have any grip (or stickiness), and you'll also find the name of the mat you are working with and the measurements both in cm and inches.

Inner Mat

The inner part of the mat is the sticky part, and it's where you lay your projects before you cut them.

The inner part of the mat is divided by 1x1in squares; this is quite handy because when you are going to cut something, you can visually know where your material is located at all times.

What are the differences between Cricut Mats?

Depending on the materials you want to work with, you will need a different type of mat.

You need to memorize, or at least have an idea of which mat you should use because Cricut Design Space will not specify you which mat you need to use for different types of materials (It will tell you what blade to use though).

With that said, it's always a good idea to have them all on hand, so you can cut anything that your heart desires!

Light Grip – Blue Mat

This mat was designed to cut lightweight materials.

If you place a thin material on a stronger grip mat, it will be pretty much impossible for you to remove that material from the mat.

The most common materials you can cut with the LightGrip mat are:

- Normal paper
- Thin cardstock
- Construction paper
- Regular vinyl

StandardGrip – Green Mat

The StandardGrip mat is the most common and affordable one, and it's designed to work with medium-weight materials.

It usually comes with the purchase of any Cricut Machine (Make sure to check out the product description though), and it's green.

The most common materials you can cut with the StandardGrip or Green mat are:

- Cardstock
- HTV (Heat Transfer Vinyl)
- Permanent or removable vinyl

Strong Grip – Purple Mat

This mat was designed to hold heavy materials in place.

Sometimes, when you are using a heavy material like balsa basswood, the grip strength is not enough. In those cases, use painters' tape to secure the material to the mat.

The most common materials you can cut with the StrongGrip mat are:

- Thick and glitter cardstock
- Balsa and basswood
- Chipboard
- Posterboard
- Leather

Fabric Grip – Pink Mat

The Pink mat the newest mat, and it came out with the release of the Cricut Maker.

The FabricGrip mat is specifically designed to cut fabric. Bonded with any of the Cricut explore Family machines or just on its own with the Rotary blade and the Cricut Maker.

The most common materials you can cut with the Strong Grip Mat are:

- Bonded fabric (Explore family machine)
- Any type of fabric with the rotary blade and Cricut Maker

Cricut Joy Mats

With the Cricut Joy, materials labeled with the word "Smart" don't need a Cricut mat. However, other materials like cardstock and regular vinyl need a mat to be cut.

The Cricut Joy has three different types of mats.

- **Light Grip Mat – Blue:** Use for thin materials like copy paper, adhesive vinyl, and iron-on.
- **Strandard Grip Mat – Green:** Use for medium weight materials like glitter cardstock, Infusible Ink, glitter iron-on, corrugated cardboard
- **Card Mat:** Use with insert cards. You can also use your paper and cut it the same size as the insert cards.

The Light Grip and the Standard Grip mat come in two sizes 4.5 x 6.5 in and 4.5 x 12 in.

Note: When you're cutting with a mat (blue or green), your design can't be larger than 4.25 x 6.25/11.75 in. And when using the Card Mat, your design can't be larger than 4.25 x 6 in.

What are the ideal projects for different mat sizes?

All of the Cricut mats come in two different sizes, 12 x 12 and 12 x 24 inches.

If you are planning to cut the same design multiple times or make something that is bigger than 12 x 12 inches, then you should get the 12 x 24 inches mat size.

Let's say you got the Cricut maker because wood and Fabric are your jam. With the 12 x 24 inches mats, you can cut bigger sizes of wood to decorate your home. The same applies to fabric; you could cut big pieces of Fabric and later sew a throw pillow cover.

Buying Mats

You can buy the mats in every craft store, on the Official Cricut Site or on amazon

How to care for and clean Cricut Mats

Taking good care of your mat is very important to ensure that your cuts are always nice and smooth.

By showing your mats some extra love, you will extender their life and save money in the long run

Here are some of the best ways you can accomplish that:

Cover it after every use

Don't ever throw away your protective cover, If you do, you will expose your mat to tons of dust and debris, and this will result in making your mat less sticky over time.

Every time you are done with the cutting and removing process, cover and put it away.

Use Cricut Mats with the right materials

Every mat is designed to be used with different materials. If you mess this up, you will have a tough time to remove them.

For instance, if you place light materials on the purple mat, you will have a tough time trying to get out that material, and this will add extra wear and tear to your mat.

The same applies to the way remove things from the mat. Be careful and try to remove elements with care and be patient.

Clean your mats often:

With time your mat will lose its grip; sometimes, there are built-up materials on it, and sometimes it's just time for you to replace it.

Before you get a new mat, try to clean it. Here are three different ways you can clean them.

Light, Strong and Standard Grip

Use the Scraper

After each use, use the scraper to remove pieces of paper.

Lint Roller

use a lint roller to get little bits of materials left on the mat. This tip works great when you need to remove Fabric!

Non-alcohol baby wipes

For just a quick clean, you can always use some baby wipes; this works like a charm if your mat has just a little dirt.

Soapy water

For deep cleaning, you can always use a washcloth with soapy water. Make sure you use lukewarm or cold water because hot water can mess up your mat's grip.

If your cleaning involves water and your mat is wet, make sure to let the mat air dry.

Fabric Mat:

The Pink Mat is very peculiar, and it requires a different type of care than the other mats!

Here are some of the best practices for cleaning and caring for the Cricut Fabric Mat

Don't use the Scraper

Don't use the scraper because the adhesive of this mat is just right to hold fabrics, and it's quite light; therefore, the scraper will peel off the grip.

Use the lint roller

Use the lint roller to get rid of some of the Fabric left on your mat.

Use transfer tape

Don't use soap or water

Don't use soap or water on this particular mat.

Keep your finger away

When manipulating your mat to place fabrics on it, make sure to keep your fingers off the grip.

Cover it

Cover it after each use.

Design Space

Now that we know what a Cricut is and how it works we can deepen how to create a design; what materials are needed and what Cricut to buy

Cricut design space is the main software to be used with the machine and now we will explain how to use it: See, when you have a clear concept of what every icon and panel is for, then you can truly dig in and start exploring further and further. Sometimes we are quick to jump from project to project – Hey That's ok too! BTDT – But I think that knowing your work area will help you to take your creativity to a whole new level.

Before we dig in, let's learn what the Cricut Design Space Canvas Area is: The Cricut Design Space Canvas Area is where all of the magic happens before you cut your projects.

Design Space is where you touch up and organize your creations. In this space, not only you can use and upload your fonts and images, but you can also use Cricut's premium images and fonts via individual purchases, Cricut Access, and Cartridges.

Investing in a Cricut is futile if you don't learn how to master Design Space because you will always need this software to cut any project. Cricut Design Space is an excellent tool for beginners, and if you have no experience with any other Design programs like

Photoshop or Illustrator, you will find that although it looks overwhelming, it's quite easy.

On the other hand, if you have preview experience with any of the Adobe Creative Cloud apps or Inkscape. You will see that this program is just a breeze. Design Space, it's mainly to touch up your projects and create minimal designs with Shapes and Fonts.

If you want something more sophisticated, you are going to need your own designs or Cricut Access. That's a membership where you get access to their supergiant library. When you log into your Cricut Design Space account and want to start or edit a new project, you will do everything from a window called CANVAS

The Canvas Area in Cricut Design Space is where you do all of your editing before you cut your projects.

The top panel in the Design Space Canvas area is for editing and arranging elements on the canvas area. From this panel, you can choose what type of font you'd like to use; you can change sizes, align designs, and more!

This panel is divided into two sub-panels. The first one allows you to save, name, and finally cut your projects. And the second one will enable you to control and edit things on the canvas area.

Sub-panel 1 Name your project and cut it

This sub-panel allows you to navigate from the Canvas to your profile, projects, and it also sends your completed projects to cut.

When you click the **"toggle menu"** button, another whole menu will slide open. This menu is a handy one. But it's not part of the Canvas, and that's why I won't be going into a lot of detail.

Basically, from here you can go to your profile and change your photo.

There are other useful and technical things you can do from this Menu like calibrating your machine, blades; also updating the Firmware – Software – of your device.

You can also manage your subscriptions from Cricut Access, your account details, and more.

Note: On the settings option, you can change the visibility and measurements of the Canvas; this is explained better at the end

Project name

All projects start with an *Untitled "title," you can only name a project from the canvas area after you've placed at least one element (Image, shape, etc.).

My Projects

When you click on my projects, you will be redirected to your library of things you have already created; this is great because sometimes you might want to re-cut a previously created project. So, there's no need for you to recreate the same project over and over.

Save

This option will activate after you've placed one element on your canvas area. I recommend you save your project as you go.

Although the software is on the cloud, if your browser crashes, there goes your hard work with it!

Maker – Explore

Depending on the type of machine you have you will need to select either the Cricut Joy, Maker or the Cricut Explore Machine; this is very important because on the Cricut Maker you will find options that are only available to that particular machine.

So, if you have a Maker and you are designing with the Explore option ON you won't be able to activate the tools that are for the maker.

Make it

When you are done uploading your files, and ready to cut click on Make it! Your projects are divided by mats according to the colours of your project.

From this window, you can also increase the number of projects to cut; this is great if you are planning on creating more than one cut.

Sub-panel 2- editing menu

It's extremely useful, and it will help you to edit, arrange, and organize fonts and images on the Canvas Area

Undo & redo

Sometimes while we work, we make mistakes. These little buttons are a great way to correct them.

Click Undo when you create something you don't like, or make a mistake. Click Redo when you accidentally delete something you didn't want to delete or modify.

Line type and Fill

This option will tell your machine what tools and blades you are going to use.

Keep in mind that depending on the Machine you have selected on the top of the window (Maker, Explore, or Joy), you will have different options.

Line type

This option will tell your machine when you are cutting your project, what tool you will be using. Right now, there are eight options (Cut, Draw, Score, Engrave, Deboss, Wave, Perf, and Foil).

If you have a Cricut Maker, all options will be available; if you have an Explore, you will be able to Cut, Draw, Score, and foil; last, if you have a Cricut Joy, only Cut and Draw will be available.

Here is a more in-depth explanation of each tool.

Cut

Unless you uploaded a JPEG or PNG image to the Canvas; "Cut" is the default linetype that all of your elements on your canvas will have; this means that when you press MAKE IT, your machine will cut those designs.

With the Cut option selected, you can change the fill of your elements, at the end of the day, this translates in the different colours of materials you will use when you cut your projects.

Draw

If you want to write on your designs, you can do it with your Cricut!

When you assign this linetype, you will be prompted to choose any of the Cricut Pens you have (You need specific pens, unless you have a 3rd party adapter). When you select a particular design, the layers on your canvas area will be outlined with the colour of the pen you picked.

With this tool, when you click Make it, instead of cutting, your Cricut will write or draw. Note: This option DOESN'T color your designs.

Score

Score is a more potent version of the Scoring line located on the left panel. When you assign this attribute to a layer, all of the designs will appear scored or dashed.

This time, when you click on Make it. Your Cricut won't cut, but it will score your materials.

For these types of projects, you will need the scoring stylus or the scoring wheel. However, keep in mind The wheel only works with the Cricut Maker.

Engrave

Allows you to engrave different types of materials. For instance, you can create monograms on aluminium sheets or anodized aluminium to reveal the silver beneath.

Deboss

This tip will push the material in, and it will create beautiful and detailed designs. The debossing tip will allow you to customize your designs to a whole new level.

Just imagine debossing a beautiful gift box with flowers, hearts, stars, etc.!

Wave

Instead of cutting on straight lines like the rotary or fine point blade, this tool will create wavy effects on your final cuts.

Getting curved lines in Design Space is quite complicated, so this tool will come in handy if you like these sorts of effects.

Perf

The Perforation Blade is a tool that allows you to cut your materials in small and uniform lines to create perfect and crisp tear effects like the ones you see in raffle tickets, coupons, tear-out cards, etc.

Foil (New)

Foil is the newest Cricut tool and it allows you to make beautiful foil finishes on your projects with the Cricut foil transfer kit.

When using this linetype you have the option to choose between fine, medium, and bold finishes.

Fill

The fill option is mainly to be used for printing and patterns.

It will only be activated when you have Cut as a "linetype." **No Fill** means that you won't be printing anything.

Print is by far, one of the best features Cricut has because it allows you to print your designs and then cut them; this is fabulous, and honestly, it's what motivated me to get a Cricut in the first place.

When this Fill option is active, after you click Make it; first, you'll send your files to your home printer and then have your Cricut do all the heavy lifting. (Cutting)

Let's say it's Valentine's Day. You can make a beautiful card with an already created pattern from Cricut Access (Membership, not free), or your own. Then print and cut at the same time.

Fill for Print then Cut ONLY works with the Cricut Maker and any of the Explore Family Machines (it's not compatible with Cricut Joy).

Select all

When you need to move all of your elements inside the canvas area, you may struggle to select them one by one.

Click Select all to select all of the elements from the canvas.

Edit

This icon will allow you to cut (remove from the canvas), copy (copy the same item, leave original intact), and paste (insert copied or cut elements on the canvas area) items from the canvas.

The Edit Icon has a drop-down menu.

The cut and copy option will be activated when you use have a selection of one or more elements from the canvas area. The Paste option will be enabled once you copy or cut something.

Align

If you have previews experience with other graphic design programs, most likely you'll know how to use this menu.

If you aren't familiar with the Align Tools, let me tell you something; the Align Menu is something that you want to master to perfection.

Align: This function allows you to align all of your designs, and it's activated when selecting two or more elements.

- – **Align Left:** When using this setting, all of the elements will be aligned to the left. The furthest element to the left will dictate where all of the other elements will move towards.

- – **Center Horizontal:** This option will align your elements horizontally; this will entirely center text and images.

- – **Align Right:** When using this setting, all of your elements will be aligned to the right. The furthest element to the right will dictate where all of the other elements will move.

- – **Align Top:** This option will align all of your selected designs to the top. The furthest element to the top will dictate where all of the other elements will move.

- – **Center Vertically:** This option will align your elements vertically. It's handy when you are working with columns, and you want them organized and aligned.

- – **Align Bottom:** This option will align all of your selected designs to the bottom. The furthest element to the bottom will dictate where all of the other elements will move.

- – **Center:** This option is a very cool one. When you click on "center," you are centering, both vertically and horizontally, one design against another one; this is particularly useful when you want to center text with a shape like a square or a star.

Distribute: If you want the same spacing between elements, it's very time consuming to do it all on your own, and it's not 100% right. The distribute button will help you out with that. For it to be activated, you must have at least three elements selected.

- – **Distribute Horizontally:** This button will distribute the elements horizontally. The furthest left and right designs will determine the length of the distribution; this means that the items that are in the center will be distributed between the most distant left and right designs.

- – **Distribute Vertically:** This button will distribute the elements vertically. The furthest top and bottom designs will determine the length of the distribution; this means that the items that are in the center will be distributed between the most distant top and bottom designs.

Arrange

When you work with multiple images, text, and designs, the new creations you add to the canvas will always be in front of everything. However, some of the elements of your design need to be in the back or front.

With the arrange option, you can organize the elements very easily.

Something great about this function is that the program will know what item is on the front or back and, and when you select it,

Design space will activate the available options for that particular element.

These are the options you get:

- – **Send to back:** This will move the selected element all the way to the back.
- – **Move Backward:** This option will move selected the item just one step back. So, if you have a three-element design. It will be like the cheese in a cheese sandwich.
- – **Move Forward:** This option will move the element just one step forward. Typically, you would use this option when you have four or more items you need to organize.
- – **Sent to front:** This option will move the selected element all the way to the front.

Flip

If you need to reflect any of your designs in Cricut Design Space, this is a great way to do it.

There are 2 options:

- – **Flip Horizontal:** This will reflect your image or design horizontally. Sort of like a mirror; It's handy when you are trying to create left and right designs. Example: You are building some wings, and already have the left side; with Flip, you can copy and paste the left wing, and voila! Now you have both (left and right) wings!
- – **Flip Vertical:** This will flip your designs vertically. Kind of like you would see your reflection on the water. If you want to create a shadow effect, this option would be great for you.

Size

Everything you create or type in Cricut Design Space has a size. You can modify the size from the element in self (when you click on it). However, if you need an item to have an exact measurement, this option will allow you to do so.

Something essential is the little lock. When you increase or reduce the size of an image, the proportions are always locked. By clicking on the small lock, you are telling the program that you don't want to keep the same dimensions.

Rotate

Just like size, rotating an element is something you can do very quickly from the canvas area. However, some designs need to be turned on a specific angle. If that's the case for you, I recommend you to use this function. Otherwise, you will spend so much time fighting to get an element angled the way you want it to be.

Position

This box shows you where your items are on the canvas area when you click on a specific design.

You can move your elements around by specifying where you want that element to be located on the canvas areas. It's handy, but it's a more advanced tool.

Font

When you click on this panel, you can select any font you want to use for your projects. You can filter them and search for them on the top of the window.

If you have Cricut Access, you can use any of all the fonts that have a little green A at the beginning of the font title.

However, if you don't have Cricut access, make sure you use your system's fonts; otherwise you will be charged when you send your project to cut.

Style

Once you pick your font, you have the option to change its form.

Some of the options you have:

- – **Regular:** this is the default setting, and it won't change the appearance of your font.
- – **Bold:** it will make the font thicker.
- – **Italic:** it will tilt the font to the right.
- – **Bold italic:** it will make the font thicker and tilt to the right.

Font, Size, Letter & Line Space

Font Size: You can change it manually from here. I usually just adjust the size of my fonts from the canvas area.

Letter Space: Some fonts have a considerable gap between each letter. This option will allow you to reduce the space between letters very quickly. It's seriously a game-changer.

Line Space: this option will tackle the space between lines in a paragraph; this is very useful because sometimes I am forced to create a single line of text because I am not happy with the spacing between lines.

Alignment

This Alignment differs from the other "alignment" I explained above. This option is for paragraphs.

These are the options you have:

- – **Left:** Align a paragraph to the left
- – **Center:** Align a paragraph to the center
- – **Right:** Align a paragraph to the right.

Curve

This option will allow you to get extra creative with your text! With this function, you can curve your text — the best way to learn it's by playing with the little slider.

When you move the slider to the left, it will curve the text upwards; and when you move it to the right, it will bend the text inwards.

Note: if you move the slider entirely to the left, or right; you will form a circle with your fonts.

Advance

Advance is the last option on the editing panel.

Don't be intimidated by the name of this drop-down menu. Once you learn what all of the options are for, you will see they are not that hard to use.

- – **Ungroup to Letters:** This option will allow you to separate each letter, into a single layer (I will explain more about Layers down below); use this, if you have plans to modify every single character.
- – **Ungroup to Lines:** This option is exceptional, and it will allow you to separate a paragraph on individual lines. Type your paragraph, then click on ungroup to lines and there you have it; a separate line that you can now modify.

- • – **Ungroup to Layers:** This one is the trickiest of all of these options. This option is only available for Multi-Layer fonts; these kinds of fonts are only available for individual purchases and, or Cricut Access.

A multi-layer font is a type of font that has more than one layer; these fonts are great if you want to have some shadow or colour around it.

What if you like a font that is multi-layer and you don't want the added layer? Just select your text and then click on ungroup to layers to separate every single layer.

Left panel – insert shapes, images & more

With the top panel you are going to edit all of your designs.

But where do they all come from? They all come from the Cricut Design Space Left Panel.

This panel is all about inserting shapes, images, ready to cut projects, and more. From here you are going to add all of the things you are going to cut.

This panel has seven options:

- • – **New:** to create and replace a new project in the canvas area.
- • – **Templates:** this allows you to have a guide on the types of things you are going to cut. Let's say you want to iron on vinyl on a onesie. When you select the template, you can design and see how the design would look like.
- • – **Projects:** Add ready to cut projects from Cricut Access.

- • – **Images:** Pick single images from Cricut Access, and cartridges to create a project.
- • – **Text:** Click here to add text on your canvas area.
- • – **Shapes:** Insert all kinds of shapes on the canvas.
- • – **Uploads:** Upload your images and cut files to the program.

There's something fundamental that you need to consider on this panel; unless you have Cricut Access, Cricut Images, ready to cut projects, and Cricut fonts cost money. If you use them, you will have to pay before you cut your project.

Now, that we saw a little preview of what everything was for on this panel. Let's see what happens when you click on each of those buttons.

New

When you click on NEW, and if you are already working on a project, you will receive a warning on top of the window asking you whether you want to replace your project or not.

If you want to replace your project, make sure to save all the changes from the current project; otherwise, you will lose all that hard work. After you save, a fresh new and empty canvas will open up for you to get started.

Templates

Templates help you to visualize and see how your project will fit on a particular surface. I think this feature is just out of this world.

If you want to personalize fashion items, this tool is marvellous because you can select sizes and different types of clothing. Plus, they also have a lot of various categories that you can choose from.

Note: templates are just for you to visualize. Nothing will be cut when you finish designing and send your project to be cut.

Projects

If you wish to cut right away, then Projects is where you want to go! Once you select your project, you can customize it; or click on make it, and follow the cutting instructions.

Tip: Most of the projects are available for Cricut Access members, or you can purchase them as you go. However, there are a handful of projects FREE for you to cut, depending on the machine you have. Just scroll to the bottom of the categories' drop-down menu and select the device you own.

Images

Images are perfect when you are putting together your own projects; with them, you can add an extra touch and personality to your crafts.

You can search by keyword, highlighted categories, themes, people, places, occasions

Cartridges are a set of images that you need to purchase separately; some of them come with Cricut Access, and some not. (Brands such as Disney, Sesame Street, Hello Kitty, etc. are not part of Cricut Access)

Under "Highlighted Categories" Cricut has FREE images to cut every week.

Anytime you click under any category a more powerful filter will appear. With this filter you can narrow your search even further.

Text

Anytime you want to type on the Canvas Area, you will need to click on Text; then, a little window that says "Add text here" will open on the canvas.

Shapes

Being able to use shapes, it's essential! With them, you can create simple and less complicated, and (also) beautiful projects.

There're nine shapes you can choose from:

- – Square
- – Triangle
- – Pentagon
- – Hexagon
- – Star
- – Octagon
- – Heart

The last option is not a shape, but an amazing and powerful tool called Score Line. With this option, you can create folds and score your materials.

If you want to create boxes or love everything about card making, the Score Line will be your best friend!

Upload

With this option, you can upload your files and images. The internet is filled with them; there are tons of bloggers that create projects for free.

Right Panel – Learn all about the layers

Layers represent every single element or design that is on the canvas area.

Think of it like clothing; when you get dressed, you have multiple layers that make up your outfit; and depending on the day, or time of year, your outfit can be simple or complex.

So, for a freezing day, your layers would be underwear, pants, shirt, jacket, sock, boots, gloves, etc.; and for a day at the pool, you would only have one layer, a Swim Suit!

The same happens with a design; depending on the complexity of the project you are working on, you'll have different types of layers that'll make up your entire project.

For example, let's pretend that you are designing a Christmas Card.

What would this card have?

Maybe a text that says Merry Christmas, a tree, the card itself, perhaps an envelope as well?

The point is that all of the little designs and elements that are part of that project are layers.

Some layers can be modified; However, other layers, like JPEG and PNG images, can't; this is because of the nature of the file or the layer itself.

For instance, a text layer can be converted into other types of layers; but, when you do that, you'll lose the ability to edit that text.

As you go, you will learn more about what can or can't do with layers.

Now let's learn what every single icon is for on this right panel.

Group, Ungroup, Duplicate and Delete

These settings will make your life easy when moving things around the canvas area, so make sure to play around with them.

Group: Click here to group layers. This setting is handy when you have different layers that make up a complex design.

Let's say you are working on an elephant. Most likely (and if this is an SVG or cut file) the elephant will be composed of different layers (the body, eyes, legs, trunk, etc.); If you want to incorporate, extra shapes, and text; most likely is that you will be moving your elephant across the canvas area a lot.

Therefore, by grouping all of the elephant layers, you can make sure that everything will stay organize and nothing will get out of place when you move them around then canvas.

Ungroup: This option will ungroup any grouped layers you select on the canvas area or layers panel. Use this option if you need to edit (size, type of font, etc.) a particular element or layer from the group.

Duplicate: This option will duplicate any layers or designs you have selected on the layers panel or canvas.

Delete: This option will delete any elements you have selected on the canvas or layers panel.

Line type/ Fill

Every item on the Layers Panel will show what Line type or Fill you are using (Cut, Write, Score, Perf, Wavy, Print, etc.).

Layer Visibility

The little eye that appears on every layer on the layers panel represents the visibility of a design. When you are not sure whether an element looks good, instead of deleting it, click on the little eye to hide that design. Note: When you hide an item, the eye will have a cross mark.

Tip: By clicking on a layer and dragging it, you can move a particular design on top or under; you could say that this works like the Arrange option (sent to the front, back, etc.).

Blank Canvas

This "layer" allows you to change the colour of your canvas; if you are trying to see how a particular design looks with a different color. The power of this setting is unleashed when you use it along with the Templates tool because you can modify the color and the options of the template itself.

Slice, Weld, Attach, Flatten and contour

These tools you see here are incredibly important! So make sure you master them to perfection.

Slice

The slice tool is perfect for cutting out shapes, text, and other elements, from different designs.

Weld

The welding tool allows you to combine two or more shapes in one.

Attach

Attach works like grouping layers, but it's more powerful.

Flatten

This tool is extra support for the Print then Cut Fill setting; when you change the fill from no fill to print, that applies to just one layer. But what if you wish to do it to multiple shapes at the time?

When you are done with your design, select the layers you want to print together as a whole, and then click on flatten.

When you are done with your designed (you can't reverse this after exiting your project), select the layers you want to print together as a whole, and then click on flatten.

Contour

The Contour tool allows you to hide unwanted pieces of a design, and it will only be activated when a shape or design has elements that can be left out.

Color Sync

Color Sync is the last option of the layers panel.

Every colour on your canvas area represents a different material colour. If your design has multiple shades of yellows or blues; are you sure you need them?

If you only need one shade of yellow just click and drag the tone you want to get rid of and drop it on the one you want to keep.

Canvas Area

The canvas area is where you see all of your designs and elements. It's very intuitive and effortless to use!

Canvas Grid and Measurements

The canvas area is divided by a grid; this is great because every little square you see on the Grid helps you to visualize the cutting mat. In the end, this will help you to maximize your space.

You can change the measurements from inches to cm and turn the grid on and off when you click on the top panel toggle and then select Settings. A window will pop up with all of the options.

Selection

Anytime you select one or more layers, the selection is blue, and you can modify it from all of the four corners.

The "red x" is for deleting the layers. The right upper corner will allow you to rotate the image (although if you need a specific angle, I recommend you to use the rotate tool on the editing menu).

The lower right button of the selection, "the small lock," keeps the size proportional when you increase or decrease the size of your layer. By clicking on it, you are now able to have different proportions.

Zoom in and Zoom Out

Last but not least. If you want to see in a bigger or smaller scale (without modifying the real size of your designs), you can do it by pressing the "+ and -" signs on the lower-left corner of the canvas.

Materials

Cricut Explorer

A Cricut Explore machine can cut pretty much anything as long as it is 2.0mm thick or thinner. And if you have a Cricut Maker, that machine has 10x the cutting force and can cut materials up to 2.4mm thick!

Cardstock and Paper

The Cricut is great at cutting paper and cardstock, but it doesn't just cut scrapbook paper! Check out all the different kinds of paper a Cricut machine can cut:

- Adhesive Cardstock
- Cardstock
- Cereal Box
- Construction Paper
- Copy Paper
- Flat Cardboard
- Flocked Cardstock
- Flocked Paper
- Foil Embossed Paper
- Foil Poster Board
- Freezer Paper

- Glitter Cardstock
- Glitter Paper
- Kraft Board
- Kraft Paper
- Metallic Cardstock
- Metallic Paper
- Metallic Poster Board
- Notebook Paper
- Paper Grocery Bags
- Parchment Paper
- Paper Board
- Pearl Cardstock
- Pearl Paper
- Photographs
- Photo Framing Mat
- Post Its
- Poster Board
- Rice Paper
- Scrapbook Paper
- Shimmer Paper
- Solid Core Cardstock
- Watercolor Paper
- Wax Paper
- White Core Cardstock

Vinyl

Another great material that the Cricut machine can cut is vinyl. Vinyl is awesome for making signs, decals, stencils, graphics, etc.

- Adhesive Vinyl
- Chalkboard Vinyl
- Dry Erase Vinyl
- Glitter Vinyl
- Glossy Vinyl
- Holographic Vinyl
- Matte Vinyl
- Metallic Vinyl
- Outdoor Vinyl
- Printable Vinyl
- Stencil Vinyl

Iron On

Iron on vinyl, also known as heat transfer vinyl. You can use iron on vinyl to decorate t-shirts, tote bags, or any other fabric item.

- Flocked Iron On
- Foil Iron On
- Glitter Iron On
- Glossy Iron On
- Holographic Sparkle Iron On
- Matte Iron On
- Metallic Iron On
- Neon Iron On
- Printable Iron On

Fabrics and Textiles

The Cricut does a great job at cutting fabrics, but you definitely want to add a stabilizer like Wonder Under or Heat'n Bond before cutting. These fabrics and textiles can be cut with a Cricut Explore machine, but there are even more that you can cut with the rotary blade on a Cricut Maker machine

- Burlap
- Canvas
- Cotton Fabric
- Denim
- Duck Cloth
- Faux Leather
- Faux Suede
- Felt
- Flannel
- Leather
- Linen
- Metallic Leather
- Oil Cloth
- Polyester
- Printable Fabric
- Silk
- Wool Felt

Other Materials

Besides fabric, paper, and vinyl, there are tons of other specialty materials a Cricut can cut as well. Here are a bunch of fun ideas!

- Adhesive Foil

- Adhesive Wood
- Aluminum Sheets
- Aluminum Foil
- Balsa Wood
- Birch Wood
- Cork Board
- Corrugated Paper
- Craft Foam
- Duct Tape
- Embossable Foil
- Foil Acetate
- Glitter Foam
- Magnet Sheets
- Metallic Vellum
- Paint Chips
- Plastic Packaging
- Printable Magnet Sheets
- Printable Sticker Paper
- Shrink Plastic
- Soda Can
- Stencil Material
- Tissue Paper
- Temporary Tattoo Paper
- Transparency Film
- Vellum
- Washi Sheets
- Washi Tape

- Window Cling
- Wood Veneer
- Wrapping Paper

Cricut Maker

If you have the Maker, you can cut even more things! The Cricut Maker has 10x the cutting force of the Explore machines, plus it has a rotary blade and a knife blade that allow it to cut even more materials. The Cricut Maker can cut materials up to 2.4mm thick, plus over 125+ types of fabric, including

- Chiffon
- Cashmere
- Fleece
- Jersey
- Jute
- Knits
- Moleskin
- Muslin
- Seersucker
- Terry Cloth
- Tulle
- Tweed
- Velvet

The end?

Now you have everything you need to create all the great design you can imagine.

Armed with machines, blade, mats, application, materials and a lot of imagination.

Create everything you want thanks to this guide